To my Family...

MY LIFE

My Reflections, Values, Experiences and Family History

Name

To My Family: My Reflections, Values, Experiences and Family History

Copyright ©2006 Diane Roblin-Lee

Published by:
Castle Quay Books
1-1295 Wharf Street, Pickering, Ont. L1W 1A2
Tel: 416-573-3249
E-mail: info@castlequaybooks.com
www.castlequaybooks.com

Concept, layout and design by Diane Roblin-Lee
Copy editing by Marina Hofman
Front Cover Design by Diane Roblin-Lee
Back Cover by John Cowie, eyetoeye design
Printed by Transcontinental

Scripture quotations, unless otherwise indicated, are from the New International Version of the Bible, copyright ©1973, 1978, 1984 by the International Bible Society. Used by permission of Zondervan Publishers.

Library and Archives Canada Cataloguing in Publication

Lee, Diane Roblin
   To My Family - My Reflections, Values, Experiences and Family History/Diane Roblin-Lee - 1st. Ed.
ISBN 1-897186-04-5

        1. Autobiography. I. Title.

CT25.L384 2006   808'.06692   C2006-904654-9

Introduction

To My Family...My Life is a legacy workbook designed for the recording of your reflections, values, experiences and family history. A treasure from your heart to your family, it will provide guideposts for your descendants for all the years to come and allow you to preserve not only the nuts and bolts of your history, but also the essence of your personality and beliefs.

Ethical wills stem from early Biblical times. Fathers summoned their children before death to invoke blessings on them and affirm the goals and values of the family. While the earliest forms were transmitted orally, the value of written ethical legacies has become recognized in recent years.

Whether you consider yourself a writer or not, doesn't matter. It is the thoughts and information you convey that your children will value - not the punctuation or the way you write. Be yourself. Write what comes from your heart.

In the "Contents" section, you will see subjects listed with pages designated for completion. If you find you have more to say on a particular subject than space will allow, pages 140 through 150 have been left blank to accommodate your needs. At the bottom of each subject page is a "Continued on..." space to enable you to direct your readers to the particular page where you have written additional information on that topic. In case there are subjects you wish to address which have not been listed in "Contents," the extra pages will suit your needs.

You are about to begin creating one of the most enduring works of your lifetime, one for which the generations to come will always thank you. Enjoy sharing the fruits of your life!

Diane Roblin-Lee

A Favorite Photo of Me

As the new heavens and the new earth that I make will endure before me,"
declares the LORD, "so will your name and descendants endure.
(Isaiah 66:22)

I bequeath to you, my friends and family, the legacy of my life. My hope is that by learning from my experiences and the conclusions I have drawn on various subjects, you will find the best road and miss some of the pot holes. There's much wisdom beyond what I have found—but that I leave for you to discover.

Name: _____

Date: _____

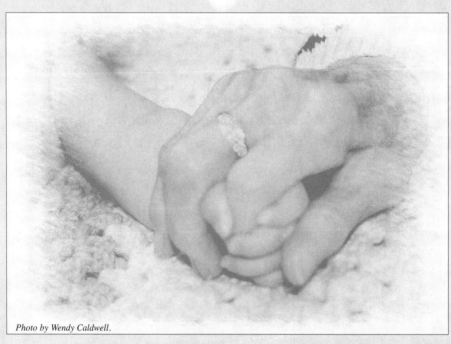

Photo by Wendy Caldwell.

Even when I am old and gray, do not forsake me,
O God, till I declare your power to the next
generation, your might to all who are to come.
(Psalm 71:18)

Contents

My son, (daughter) if you accept my words and store up my commands within you, turning your ear to wisdom and applying your heart to understanding, and if you call out for insight and cry aloud for understanding, and if you look for it as for silver and search for it as for hidden treasure, then you will understand the fear of the LORD and find the knowledge of God. For the LORD gives wisdom, and from his mouth come knowledge and understanding.

(Proverbs 2:1-6)

*All this I have told you so that you
will not go astray.*

(John 16:1)

My Blessing for my Family

Declare or pray a blessing on your family members.
Numbers 6:22-26 contains the blessing Aaron and his sons were to give the
Israelites. "The LORD said to Moses, 'Tell Aaron and his sons,
'This is how you are to bless the Israelites. Say to them:
'The LORD bless you and keep you;
the LORD make his face shine upon you and be gracious to you;
the LORD turn his face toward you and give you peace.'"
Like Abraham, we are to be channels through whom God can provide, protect and
profusely give His blessing. God wants us to transmit that blessing to our families.

_____

_____

_____

_____

_____

_____

_____

_____

_____

_____

_____

_____

_____

And he took the children in his arms, put his hands on them and blessed them.
(Mark 10:16)

Bring me some game and prepare me some tasty food to eat,
so that I may give you my blessing
in the presence of the LORD before I die.
Now, my son, listen carefully and do what I tell you.
(Genesis 27:7-8)

Oh, that my words were recorded, that they were written on a scroll, that they were inscribed with an iron tool on lead, or engraved in rock forever! I know that my Redeemer lives, and that in the end he will stand upon the earth. And after my skin has been destroyed, yet in my flesh I will see God. (Job 19:23-26)

The Story of my Life

Date of Birth:

Location of Birth:

My Cultural Heritage and Family Roots:

Mother:

Father:

Siblings:

The Story of My Life (continued)

Early Years:

_____

_____

_____

_____

_____

_____

_____

_____

_____

_____

_____

_____

_____

_____

_____

_____

_____

Childhood or Adult Baptism:

_____

_____

Blessed is the man who does not walk in the counsel of the wicked or stand in the way of sinners or sit in the seat of mockers. But his delight is in the law of the LORD, and on his law he meditates day and night. He is like a tree planted by streams of water, which yields its fruit in season and whose leaf does not wither.
Whatever he does prospers.
(Psalm 1:1-3)

Places I Have Lived:

My Education:

Military Records:

My Marriage to:

    Date: *Location:*

    Attendees:

    Reflections:

My Marriage to:

    Date: *Location:*

    Attendees:

    Reflections:

The Story of My Life (continued)

My Life's Work:

My Adult Family:

Health Issues:

My Travels:

I have seen the burden God has laid on men. He has made everything beautiful in its time. He has also set eternity in the hearts of men; yet they cannot fathom what God has done from beginning to end. I know that there is nothing better for men than to be happy and do good while they live. That everyone may eat and drink, and find satisfaction in all his toil—this is the gift of God.
(Ecclesiastes 3:10-13)

Memorable People I Have Met:

A Few of my Most Interesting Experiences:

Historical Events I Attended:

Events That Changed the Life of Our Family:

(Continued on page _____)

17

The Ancestry of my Birth Father

Father
b. _____
m. _____
d. _____

Father
b. _____
m. _____
d. _____

Father
b. _____
m. _____
d. _____

Father
b. _____
m. _____
d. _____

Mother
b. _____
m. _____
d. _____

Mother
b. _____
m. _____
d. _____

Mother
b. _____
m. _____
d. _____

Mother
b. _____
m. _____
d. _____

Father
b. _____
m. _____
d. _____

Mother
b. _____
m. _____
d. _____

Father
b. _____
m. _____
d. _____

Mother
b. _____
m. _____
d. _____

Father
b. _____
m. _____
d. _____

Mother
b. _____
m. _____
d. _____

Legend:
b. Birth Date
m. Marriage Date
d. Deceased

My Birth Father
b. _____
m. _____
d. _____

The Ancestry of my Birth Mother

Father
b. _____
m. _____
d. _____

Father
b. _____
m. _____
d. _____

Father
b. _____
m. _____
d. _____

Father
b. _____
m. _____
d. _____

Mother
b. _____
m. _____
d. _____

Mother
b. _____
m. _____
d. _____

Mother
b. _____
m. _____
d. _____

Mother
b. _____
m. _____
d. _____

Father
b. _____
m. _____
d. _____

Mother
b. _____
m. _____
d. _____

Father
b. _____
m. _____
d. _____

Mother
b. _____
m. _____
d. _____

Father
b. _____
m. _____
d. _____

Mother
b. _____
m. _____
d. _____

My Birth Mother
b. _____
m. _____
d. _____

Legend:
b. Birth Date
m. Marriage Date
d. Deceased

My Brothers

Brother #1
Born: _____
Deceased: _____

1. Spouse
Born: _____
Married: _____

Their Children:
1. Name: _____
Birthday: _____
2. Name: _____
Birthday: _____
3. Name: _____
Birthday: _____
4. Name: _____
Birthday: _____
5. Name: _____
Birthday: _____

2. Spouse
Born: _____
Married: _____

Their Children:
1. Name: _____
Birthday: _____
2. Name: _____
Birthday: _____
3. Name: _____
Birthday: _____
4. Name: _____
Birthday: _____
5. Name: _____
Birthday: _____

Brother #2
Born: _____
Deceased: _____

1. Spouse
Born: _____
Married: _____

Their Children:
1. Name: _____
Birthday: _____
2. Name: _____
Birthday: _____
3. Name: _____
Birthday: _____
4. Name: _____
Birthday: _____
5. Name: _____
Birthday: _____

2. Spouse
Born: _____
Married: _____

Their Children:
1. Name: _____
Birthday: _____
2. Name: _____
Birthday: _____
3. Name: _____
Birthday: _____
4. Name: _____
Birthday: _____
5. Name: _____
Birthday: _____

My Sisters

Sister #1	1. Spouse	2. Spouse
Born:	Born:	Born:
Deceased:	Married:	Married:

	Their Children:	Their Children:
	1. Name:	1. Name:
	Birthday:	Birthday:
	2. Name:	2. Name:
	Birthday:	Birthday:
	3. Name:	3. Name:
	Birthday:	Birthday:
	4. Name:	4. Name:
	Birthday:	Birthday:
	5. Name:	5. Name:
	Birthday:	Birthday:

Sister #2	1. Spouse	2. Spouse
Born:	Born:	Born:
Deceased:	Married:	Married:

	Their Children:	Their Children:
	1. Name:	1. Name:
	Birthday:	Birthday:
	2. Name:	2. Name:
	Birthday:	Birthday:
	3. Name:	3. Name:
	Birthday:	Birthday:
	4. Name:	4. Name:
	Birthday:	Birthday:
	5. Name:	5. Name:
	Birthday:	Birthday:

My Brothers

Brother #3	1. Spouse	2. Spouse
Born:	Born:	Born:
Deceased:	Married:	Married:

	Their Children:	Their Children:
	1. Name:	1. Name:
	Birthday:	Birthday:
	2. Name:	2. Name:
	Birthday:	Birthday:
	3. Name:	3. Name:
	Birthday:	Birthday:
	4. Name:	4. Name:
	Birthday:	Birthday:
	5. Name:	5. Name:
	Birthday:	Birthday:

Brother #4	1. Spouse	2. Spouse
Born:	Born:	Born:
Deceased:	Married:	Married:

	Their Children:	Their Children:
	1. Name:	1. Name:
	Birthday:	Birthday:
	2. Name:	2. Name:
	Birthday:	Birthday:
	3. Name:	3. Name:
	Birthday:	Birthday:
	4. Name:	4. Name:
	Birthday:	Birthday:
	5. Name:	5. Name:
	Birthday:	Birthday:

My Sisters

Sister #3
Born: _____
Deceased: _____

1. Spouse
Born: _____
Married: _____

Their Children:
1. Name: _____
Birthday: _____
2. Name: _____
Birthday: _____
3. Name: _____
Birthday: _____
4. Name: _____
Birthday: _____
5. Name: _____
Birthday: _____

2. Spouse
Born: _____
Married: _____

Their Children:
1. Name: _____
Birthday: _____
2. Name: _____
Birthday: _____
3. Name: _____
Birthday: _____
4. Name: _____
Birthday: _____
5. Name: _____
Birthday: _____

Sister #4
Born: _____
Deceased: _____

1. Spouse
Born: _____
Married: _____

Their Children:
1. Name: _____
Birthday: _____
2. Name: _____
Birthday: _____
3. Name: _____
Birthday: _____
4. Name: _____
Birthday: _____
5. Name: _____
Birthday: _____

2. Spouse
Born: _____
Married: _____

Their Children:
1. Name: _____
Birthday: _____
2. Name: _____
Birthday: _____
3. Name: _____
Birthday: _____
4. Name: _____
Birthday: _____
5. Name: _____
Birthday: _____

My Brothers

Brother #5
Born: _____
Deceased: _____

1. Spouse
Born: _____
Married: _____

Their Children:
1. Name: _____
Birthday: _____
2. Name: _____
Birthday: _____
3. Name: _____
Birthday: _____
4. Name: _____
Birthday: _____
5. Name: _____
Birthday: _____

2. Spouse
Born: _____
Married: _____

Their Children:
1. Name: _____
Birthday: _____
2. Name: _____
Birthday: _____
3. Name: _____
Birthday: _____
4. Name: _____
Birthday: _____
5. Name: _____
Birthday: _____

Brother #6
Born: _____
Deceased: _____

1. Spouse
Born: _____
Married: _____

Their Children:
1. Name: _____
Birthday: _____
2. Name: _____
Birthday: _____
3. Name: _____
Birthday: _____
4. Name: _____
Birthday: _____
5. Name: _____
Birthday: _____

2. Spouse
Born: _____
Married: _____

Their Children:
1. Name: _____
Birthday: _____
2. Name: _____
Birthday: _____
3. Name: _____
Birthday: _____
4. Name: _____
Birthday: _____
5. Name: _____
Birthday: _____

My Sisters

Sister #5

Born: _____

Deceased: _____

1. Spouse

Born: _____

Married: _____

Their Children:

1. Name: _____
Birthday: _____
2. Name: _____
Birthday: _____
3. Name: _____
Birthday: _____
4. Name: _____
Birthday: _____
5. Name: _____
Birthday: _____

2. Spouse

Born: _____

Married: _____

Their Children:

1. Name: _____
Birthday: _____
2. Name: _____
Birthday: _____
3. Name: _____
Birthday: _____
4. Name: _____
Birthday: _____
5. Name: _____
Birthday: _____

Sister #6

Born: _____

Deceased: _____

1. Spouse

Born: _____

Married: _____

Their Children:

1. Name: _____
Birthday: _____
2. Name: _____
Birthday: _____
3. Name: _____
Birthday: _____
4. Name: _____
Birthday: _____
5. Name: _____
Birthday: _____

2. Spouse

Born: _____

Married: _____

Their Children:

1. Name: _____
Birthday: _____
2. Name: _____
Birthday: _____
3. Name: _____
Birthday: _____
4. Name: _____
Birthday: _____
5. Name: _____
Birthday: _____

My Brothers

Brother #7

Born:

Deceased:

1. Spouse

Born:

Married:

2. Spouse

Born:

Married:

Their Children:

1. Name:

Birthday:

2. Name:

Birthday:

3. Name:

Birthday:

4. Name:

Birthday:

5. Name:

Birthday:

Their Children:

1. Name:

Birthday:

2. Name:

Birthday:

3. Name:

Birthday:

4. Name:

Birthday:

5. Name:

Birthday:

Brother #8

Born:

Deceased:

1. Spouse

Born:

Married:

2. Spouse

Born:

Married:

Their Children:

1. Name:

Birthday:

2. Name:

Birthday:

3. Name:

Birthday:

4. Name:

Birthday:

5. Name:

Birthday:

Their Children:

1. Name:

Birthday:

2. Name:

Birthday:

3. Name:

Birthday:

4. Name:

Birthday:

5. Name:

Birthday:

My Sisters

Sister #7

Born:

Deceased:

1. Spouse

Born:

Married:

Their Children:

1. Name:
Birthday:
2. Name:
Birthday:
3. Name:
Birthday:
4. Name:
Birthday:
5. Name:
Birthday:

2. Spouse

Born:

Married:

Their Children:

1. Name:
Birthday:
2. Name:
Birthday:
3. Name:
Birthday:
4. Name:
Birthday:
5. Name:
Birthday:

Sister #8

Born:

Deceased:

1. Spouse

Born:

Married:

Their Children:

1. Name:
Birthday:
2. Name:
Birthday:
3. Name:
Birthday:
4. Name:
Birthday:
5. Name:
Birthday:

2. Spouse

Born:

Married:

Their Children:

1. Name:
Birthday:
2. Name:
Birthday:
3. Name:
Birthday:
4. Name:
Birthday:
5. Name:
Birthday:

My Brothers

Brother #9
Born: _____
Deceased: _____

1. Spouse
Born: _____
Married: _____

Their Children:
1. Name: _____
Birthday: _____
2. Name: _____
Birthday: _____
3. Name: _____
Birthday: _____
4. Name: _____
Birthday: _____
5. Name: _____
Birthday: _____

2. Spouse
Born: _____
Married: _____

Their Children:
1. Name: _____
Birthday: _____
2. Name: _____
Birthday: _____
3. Name: _____
Birthday: _____
4. Name: _____
Birthday: _____
5. Name: _____
Birthday: _____

Brother #10
Born: _____
Deceased: _____

1. Spouse
Born: _____
Married: _____

Their Children:
1. Name: _____
Birthday: _____
2. Name: _____
Birthday: _____
3. Name: _____
Birthday: _____
4. Name: _____
Birthday: _____
5. Name: _____
Birthday: _____

2. Spouse
Born: _____
Married: _____

Their Children:
1. Name: _____
Birthday: _____
2. Name: _____
Birthday: _____
3. Name: _____
Birthday: _____
4. Name: _____
Birthday: _____
5. Name: _____
Birthday: _____

My Sisters

Sister #9
Born:
Deceased:

1. Spouse
Born:
Married:

2. Spouse
Born:
Married:

Their Children:
1. Name:
Birthday:
2. Name:
Birthday:
3. Name:
Birthday:
4. Name:
Birthday:
5. Name:
Birthday:

Their Children:
1. Name:
Birthday:
2. Name:
Birthday:
3. Name:
Birthday:
4. Name:
Birthday:
5. Name:
Birthday:

Sister #10
Born:
Deceased:

1. Spouse
Born:
Married:

2. Spouse
Born:
Married:

Their Children:
1. Name:
Birthday:
2. Name:
Birthday:
3. Name:
Birthday:
4. Name:
Birthday:
5. Name:
Birthday:

Their Children:
1. Name:
Birthday:
2. Name:
Birthday:
3. Name:
Birthday:
4. Name:
Birthday:
5. Name:
Birthday:

My Thoughts on...

The Afterlife

Just as man is destined to die once, and after that to face judgment,
so Christ was sacrificed once to take away the sins of many people;
and he will appear a second time, not to bear sin,
but to bring salvation to those who are waiting for him.
(Hebrews 9:27-28)

My Hopes and Expectations Concerning my own Afterlife...

People I Long to See who Have Gone on Before...

(Continued on page _____)

My Thoughts on...

Ageing

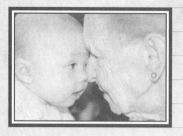

But if a widow has children or grandchildren, these should learn first of all to put their religion into practice by caring for their own family and so repaying their parents and grandparents, for this is pleasing to God.
(1Timothy 5:4)

My Personal Experience with Ageing...

(Continued on page _____)

My Thoughts on...
Animals and Pets

The wolf will live with the lamb, the leopard will lie down with the goat,
the calf and the lion and the yearling together;
and a little child will lead them.
(Isaiah 11:6)

A Few of my Favorite Animals and Pets...

(Continued on page _____)

My Thoughts on...

Books

Jesus did many other things as well. If every one of them were written down,
I suppose that even the whole world would not have room
for the books that would be written.
(John 21:25)

A Few of my Favorite Books and what I Liked About Them...

(Continued on page _____)

My Thoughts on...
Business and the Economy

You may say to yourself, "My power and the strength of my hands have produced this wealth for me." But remember the LORD your God, for it is he who gives you the ability to produce wealth...
(Deuteronomy 8:17-18)

My Experience with Business and the Economy...

_____
_____
_____
_____
_____
_____
_____
_____
_____

My Favorite or Most Noteworthy Occupations—Dates and Locations...

_____
_____
_____
_____
_____
_____
_____
_____
_____
_____
_____

(Continued on page _____)

My Thoughts on...

Education

Choose my instruction instead of silver, knowledge rather than choice gold, for wisdom is more precious than rubies, and nothing you desire can compare with her. I, wisdom, dwell together with prudence; I possess knowledge and discretion.
(Proverbs 8:10-12)

My Education and Experiences in Education...

_____

_____

_____

_____

_____

_____

My Favorite Teachers and Memories...

_____

_____

_____

_____

_____

_____

_____

_____

(Continued on page _____)

My Thoughts on...

Faith

What I Believe...

Now faith is being sure of what we hope for and certain of what we do not see.
(Hebrews 11:1)
For it is by grace you have been saved, through faith—and this not from
yourselves, it is the gift of God—not by works, so that no one can boast.
(Ephesians 2:8-9)

My Faith Experience...

_____

_____

_____

_____

_____

_____

_____

_____

Memorable Moments Associated with my Faith...

_____

_____

_____

_____

_____

_____

_____

_____

_____

_____

_____

(Continued on page _____)

My Thoughts on...
Fame and Fortune

He who pursues righteousness and love finds life,
prosperity and honor.
(Proverbs 21:21)

My Experience with Fame and Fortune...

The Most Famous People I Have Met...

(Continued on page _____)

45

My Thoughts on...

Family Life

Blessed are all who fear the LORD, who walk in His ways.
You will eat the fruit of your labor; blessings and prosperity will be yours.
Your wife will be like a fruitful vine within your house;
your sons will be like olive shoots around your table.
Thus is the man blessed who fears the LORD.
(Psalm 128:1-4)

Family Life in our Home...

(Continued on page _____)

My Thoughts on... *Finding a Career*

Tips for Being a Valuable Worker:

In his heart a man plans his course, but the LORD determines his steps.
(Proverbs 16:9)

Do not let this Book of the Law depart from your mouth;
meditate on it day and night, so that you may be careful to do everything written in it.
Then you will be prosperous and successful.
(Joshua 1:8)

How I Found my Life's Work...

_____
_____
_____
_____
_____
_____
_____
_____
_____
_____
_____

Tips for Being a Good Employer:

_____
_____
_____
_____
_____
_____
_____
_____
_____
_____
_____
_____

(Continued on page _____)

My Thoughts on...

Finding One's Mate

Delight yourself in the LORD and he will give you the desires of your heart.
(Psalm 37:4)
He who finds a wife finds what is good and receives favor from the LORD.
(Proverbs 18:22)

My Experiences Finding a Mate...

(Continued on page _____)

My Thoughts on...

Freedom

*Now the Lord is the Spirit, and where the
Spirit of the Lord is, there is freedom.
(2 Corinthians 3:17)*

My Experiences with Freedom or the Lack Thereof...

(Continued on page _____)

My Thoughts on...
Getting Along with People

For if you forgive men when they sin against you, your heavenly
Father will also forgive you. But if you do not forgive men
their sins, your Father will not forgive your sins.
(Matthew 6:14-15)
When a man's ways are pleasing to the LORD,
he makes even his enemies live at peace with him.
(Proverbs 16:7)

My Personal Experiences in Getting Along with People...

(Continued on page _____)

My Thoughts on...
Health and Home Remedies

My son, pay attention to what I say; listen closely to my words.
Do not let them out of your sight, keep them within your heart;
for they are life to those who find them and
health to a man's whole body.
(Proverbs 4:20-22)

My Health History and Favorite Home Remedies...

(Continued on page _____)

My Thoughts on...

Heroes and Mentors

He who walks with the wise grows wise,
but a companion of fools suffers harm.
(Proverbs 13:20)

My Heroes and Mentors Were...

(Continued on page _____)

My Thoughts on...
Hobbies and Leisure Time

Commit to the LORD whatever you do, and your plans will succeed.
(Proverbs 16:3)

A Few of my Hobbies Through the Years...

(Continued on page _____)

My Thoughts on...
Home and Housekeeping

He who fears the LORD has a secure fortress, and for his children it will be a refuge.
(Proverbs 14:26)
By wisdom a house is built, and through understanding it is established; through
knowledge its rooms are filled with rare and beautiful treasures.
(Proverbs 24:3-4)

My Favorite Housekeeping Tips...

Use shaving cream or club soda as instant spot remover

Make your candles by freezing them

(Continued on page _____)

My Thoughts on...
Honors and Accomplishments

Let another praise you, and not your own mouth;
someone else, and not your own lips.
(Proverbs 27:2)

My Most Notable Honors and Accomplishments...

(Continued on page _____)

My Thoughts on...

Humor

*Our mouths were filled with laughter, our tongues with
songs of joy. Then it was said among the nations,
"The LORD has done great things for them."
(Psalm 126:2)*

My Favorite Family Jokes and Humorous Stories...

(Continued on page _____)

The Laws of the Land

*The integrity of the upright guides them, but the unfaithful
are destroyed by their duplicity.
(Proverbs 11:3)
Fear the LORD and the king, my son, and do not join with the rebellious,
for those two will send sudden destruction upon them,
and who knows what calamities they can bring?
(Proverbs 24:21-22)*

The Results of my Approach to Matters of the Law...

(Continued on page _____)

My Thoughts on...

Leadership

If a man's gift is ...leadership, let him govern diligently...
(Romans 12:8)

My Experience with Leadership...

(Continued on page _____)

My Thoughts on...
Managing Money and Giving

BALANCE SHEET			
ASSETS		**LIABILITIES**	
Res. Home	$ _____	Mortgage Res.	$ _____
Other Realty	$ _____	Mortgage	$ _____
Bonds	$ _____	Credit Cards	$ _____
Stocks	$ _____		$ _____
Bank Savings	$ _____		$ _____
Investments Total	$ _____	Business Loans	$ _____
Business Interest	$ _____		$ _____
Cash Val. Life Ins.	$ _____		$ _____
R.R.S.P.s	$ _____	Bank Loans	$ _____
Chequing Acc't.	$ _____		$ _____
Notes Receivable	$ _____	Car Loans	$ _____
Personal Property	$ _____		$ _____
Boats, Autos etc.	$ _____	Notes Payable	$ _____
Royalties, etc.	$ _____		$ _____
Other assets	$ _____	Other Debts	$ _____
	$ _____		$ _____
TOTAL ASSETS	$ _____	**TOTAL LIAB.**	$ _____

Whoever sows sparingly will also reap sparingly,
and whoever sows generously will also reap generously.
(2 Corinthians 9:6)
Honor the LORD with your wealth, with the firstfruits of all your crops; then your
barns will be filled to overflowing, and your vats will brim over with new wine.
(Proverbs 3:9-10)

My Personal Money Management Plan...

(Continued on page _____)

My Thoughts on...
Marriage and Divorce

A wife of noble character is her husband's crown,
but a disgraceful wife is like decay in his bones.
(Proverbs 12:4)
Husbands, love your wives, just as Christ loved the church
and gave himself up for her.
(Ephesians 5:25)

My Personal Experience with Marriage and Divorce...

(Continued on page _____)

The Military and War

You will hear of wars and rumors of wars, but see to it that you are not alarmed.
Such things must happen, but the end is still to come.
(Matthew 24:6)

My Personal Experience with the Military and War...

(Continued on page _____)

My Thoughts on...

Morality

Above all else, guard your heart, for it is the wellspring of life.
(Proverbs 4:23)
My son, if sinners entice you, do not give in to them.
(Proverbs 1:10)
He who pursues righteousness and love finds life, prosperity and honor.
(Proverbs 21:21)

My Personal Moral Compass...

(Continued on page _____)

My Thoughts on...

Music and the Arts

Sing to him a new song; play skillfully, and shout for joy.
(Psalm 33:3)

My Personal Taste and Abilities in Music and the Arts...

_____
_____
_____
_____
_____
_____
_____

My Favorite Songs...

_____
_____
_____
_____
_____
_____
_____

My Favorite Music and Artists...

_____
_____
_____
_____
_____
_____
_____

(Continued on page _____)

My Thoughts on...

Parenting

Fathers, do not exasperate your children; instead,
bring them up in the training and instruction of the Lord.
(Ephesians 6:4)
Listen to your father, who gave you life, and do not despise your mother when she is old.
(Proverbs 23:22)

My Personal Experience with Parenting...

(Continued on page _____)

My Thoughts on...
Physical Appearance and Fashion

Therefore, as God's chosen people, holy and dearly loved,
clothe yourselves with compassion, kindness,
humility, gentleness and patience.
(Colossians 3:12)
(A wise woman) is clothed with strength and dignity; she can laugh at the days to come.
(Proverbs 31:25)

How my Appearance has Affected my Life and my Personal Style...

(Continued on page _____)

My Thoughts on...
Politics and my Worldview

When the righteous thrive, the people rejoice;
when the wicked rule, the people groan.
(Proverbs 29:2)

My Personal Involvement in Matters of Government...

My Favorite Political Leaders Were...

(Continued on page _____)

87

My Thoughts on...

Possessions

How much better to get wisdom than gold,
to choose understanding rather than silver!
(Proverbs 16:16)

My Most Cherished Possessions...

(Continued on page _____)

My Thoughts on... The Purpose of Life

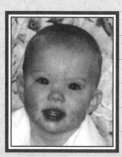

*"...For I know the plans I have for you," declares the LORD,
"plans to prosper you and not to harm you, plans
to give you hope and a future. Then you will call upon me
and come and pray to me, and I will listen to you..."*
(Jeremiah 29:11-12)

What I Believe to be God's Purpose for my own Life on Earth...

(Continued on page _____)

Qualities I Value Most in People

Let love and faithfulness never leave you; bind them around your neck,
write them on the tablet of your heart.
Then you will win favor and a good name in the sight of God and man.
(Proverbs 3:3-4)
He who loves a pure heart and whose speech is gracious
will have the king for his friend.
(Proverbs 22:11)

What I Believe to be my Best Qualities...

(Continued on page _____)

My Thoughts on...
Relatives and Friends

A friend loves at all times, and a brother is born for adversity.
(Proverbs 17:17)

My Closest Relatives and Friends...

_____
_____
_____
_____
_____
_____
_____
_____
_____
_____
_____
_____

A Few Memories of My Closest Relatives and Friends...

_____
_____
_____
_____
_____
_____
_____
_____
_____
_____
_____
_____

(Continued on page _____)

My Thoughts on...
Scriptures and Sayings

*Let the wise listen and add to their learning, and let the
discerning get guidance — for understanding proverbs and
parables, the sayings and riddles of the wise.*
(Proverbs 1:5-6)

A Few of my Favorite Scriptures and Sayings...

(Continued on page _____)

My Thoughts on...

Sports

But one thing I do: Forgetting what is behind and straining toward what is ahead,
I press on toward the goal to win the prize for which
God has called me heavenward in Christ Jesus.
(Philippians 3:13-14)
Everything is possible for him who believes.
(Mark 9:23)

My Favorite Sports and Sports Abilities...

A Few of My Favorite Athletes...

(Continued on page _____)

My Thoughts on...
Talents and Special Abilities

To one he gave five talents of money, to another two talents,
and to another one talent, each according to his ability.
(Matthew 25:15)
...Everything is possible for him who believes.
(Mark 9:23)

My Talents and Special Abilities...

(Continued on page _____)

My Thoughts on...

Traditions

And the child grew and became strong; he was filled with wisdom,
and the grace of God was upon him. Every year his parents went to
Jerusalem for the Feast of the Passover. When he was twelve years old,
they went up to the Feast, according to the custom.
(Luke 2:40-42)

Special Traditions of our Family...

(Continued on page _____)

My Thoughts on...

Travel

*And this Gospel of the Kingdom will be preached in
the whole world as a testimony to all nations,
and then the end will come.
(Matthew 24:14)*

My Most Memorable Trips...

(Continued on page _____)

The Ten Most Important
Things to Know About Life are:

1.

2.

3.

4.

5.

6.

7.

8.

9.

10.

(Continued on page _____)

A Favorite Photo of Me

Things I Would Like You to Remember About Me:

(Continued on page _____)

Old Family Stories, Legends and History

The memory of the righteous will be a blessing.
(Proverbs 10:7)

The righteous man leads a blameless life; blessed are his children after him.
(Proverbs 20:7)

Old Family Stories continued...

Gray hair is a crown of splendor; it is attained by a righteous life.
(Proverbs 16:31)

Children's children are a crown to the aged.
(Proverbs 17:6)

Old Family Stories continued...

A wife of noble character who can find? She is worth far more than rubies.
(Proverbs 31:10)

(Continued on page _____)

A Few of My Favorite Recipes

Pleasant words are a honeycomb, sweet to the soul and healing to the bones.
(Proverbs 16:24)

(Recipes continued...)

Man does not live on bread alone,
but on every word that comes from the mouth of God.
(Matthew 4:4)

(Recipes continued...)

Daniel then said to the guard... "Please test your servants for ten days: Give us nothing but vegetables to eat and water to drink. Then compare our appearance with that of the young men who eat the royal food, and treat your servants in accordance with what you see." At the end of the ten days they looked healthier and better nourished than any of the young men who ate the royal food.
(Daniel 1:11-13,15)

(Recipes continued...)

Better a meal of vegetables where there is love than a fattened calf with hatred.
(Proverbs 15:17)

(Recipes continued...)

All the days of the oppressed are wretched,
but the cheerful heart has a continual feast.
(Proverbs 15:15)

(Recipes continued...)

*The people of Israel called the bread manna. It was white like coriander seed
and tasted like wafers made with honey.
(Exodus 16:31)*

(Recipes continued...)

A feast is made for laughter, and wine makes life merry...
(Ecclesiastes 10:19)

(Continued on page _____)

Possessions I Would Like Specific People to Have

How much better to get wisdom than gold, to choose
understanding rather than silver!
(Proverbs 16:16)

(Continued on page _____)

My Message to Specific Friends and Family

For a man's ways are in full view of the LORD, and he examines all his paths.

(Proverbs 5:21)

Things I Should Have Said—But Didn't...

(Continued on page _____)

Photos

Photos

Photos

Photos

Photos

Photos

(Continued on page _____)